Publish Your Book Promote Your Business

The Ultimate Lead Generation Tool For Professionals and Small Business Owners

V. LaTonya Cobbs

© 2014 by *V. LaTonya Cobbs*

All rights reserved.

All Rights Reserved. No part of this publication may be reproduced in any form or by any means, including scanning, photocopying, or otherwise without prior written permission of the copyright holder.

Disclaimer and Terms of Use: The Author and Publisher have strived to be as accurate and complete as possible in the creation of this book, notwithstanding the fact that she does not warrant or represent at any time that the contents within are accurate due to the rapidly changing nature of the Internet. While all attempts have been made to verify information provided in this publication, the Author and Publisher assumes no responsibility for errors, omissions, or contrary interpretation of the subject matter herein. Any perceived slights of specific persons, peoples or organizations are unintentional. In practical advice books, like anything else in life, there are no guarantees of income made. Readers are cautioned to reply on their own judgment about their individual circumstances to act accordingly. This book is not intended for use as a source of legal, business, accounting or financial advice. All readers are advised to seek services of competent professionals in legal, business, accounting, and finance field.

First Printing, 2014 Arev Media Marketing & Publishing

ISBN-13: 978-1502774064
ISBN-10: 1502774062

Printed in the United States of America

Income Disclaimer

This document contains business strategies, marketing methods and other business advice that, regardless of my own results and experience, may not produce the same results (or any results) for you. I make absolutely no guarantee, expressed or implied, that by following the advice below you will make any money or improve current profits, as there are several factors and variables that come into play regarding any given business.

Primarily, results will depend on the nature of the product or business model, the conditions of the marketplace, the experience of the individual, and situations and elements that are beyond your control.

As with any business endeavor, you assume all risk related to investment and money based on your own discretion and at your own potential expense.

Liability Disclaimer

By reading this document, you assume all risks associated with using the advice given below, with a full understanding that you, solely, are responsible for anything that may occur as a result of putting this information into action in any way, and regardless of your interpretation of the advice.

You further agree that our company cannot be held responsible in any way for the success or failure of your business as a result of the information presented below. It is your responsibility to conduct your own due diligence regarding the safe and successful operation of your business if you intend to apply any of our information in any way to your business operations.

Terms of Use

You are given a non-transferable, "personal use" license to this product. You cannot distribute it or share it with other individuals.

Also, there are no resale rights or private label rights granted when purchasing this document. In other words, it's for your own personal use only.

Dedication

To Jesse, my muse without whom I would have never finished this project. You believe in me and encourage me even when I can't find faith in myself and for that I am forever grateful.

To my children, Davico Jr., Danisha, Te' Sharra & DaVon. I love you all more than any words could ever express (I play with words for a living so trust me there aren't any). I want to thank the four of you for believing that mommy can do anything, as it turns out you were right.

To Kellie, my favorite cousin, I love you and I truly appreciate the person that you are. You push me to greatness no matter how much I resist and you never let me accept failure. For this, I know that I am truly blessed.

Publish Your Book Promote Your Business

The Ultimate Lead Generation Tool For Professionals and Small Business Owners

Contents

Introduction 1
Why Would I Write a Book 3
Types of Books to Write 7
How do I Write a Book if I'm Not a Writer..... 11
Putting Your Book Together 15
Now Is the Perfect Time to Publish Your Book
.... 27
Enhancing Your Credibility Through Book
Promotion.. 43
Generating Leads With Your Book 51
Take Action Now 54
About The Author.. 55
Have the Author Speak at Your Next Event 56
Done-For-You Book Service 57
Readers Only Bonus 58

Introduction

Welcome and thank you for grabbing a copy of ***Publish Your Book Promote Your Business: The Ultimate Lead Generation Tool For Professionals and Small Business Owners.*** This book was written for professionals, entrepreneurs and small business owners who are looking for effective lead generation methods and may have considered writing a book to promote themselves and their business but don't know how or where to start. It was also written for those who may be asking the question "I'm not an author, why would I want to write a book?" I intend to answer that question within these pages.

We are in the most exciting time in human history, we have the ability to not only communicate with the entire connected planet but to also build relationships with people all over the globe. We are no longer confined to our own backyards and so what that means for you and your business is that you can reach potential clients anywhere in the world and build long-term business relationships with them.

This is excellent news if you are a coach, consultant or other service oriented professional because thanks to the Internet and the new self-publishing era, you can actually get your message out and make your mark on the world without worrying about the limitations of travel and physical location. Your market reach just got a whole lot bigger, and you now have the ability to put your message into the hands of that market without the restrictions and politics of old outdated publishing processes.

To the best of my ability, I have included everything necessary to dispel any myths about writing a book for business purposes and to give you the tools you need to write, publish and market a successful lead generating book. Just keep in mind that this book is not all-encompassing and methods as well as resources do change from time to time. In the event that some information needs to be updated you can find these updates at the book's website www.publishyourbookpromoteyourbusiness.com. You can also contact me, leave comments or ask any questions on the book's website.

Why Would I Write a Book

If you are a professional, coach, consultant, speaker or small business owner that provides services of any kind, you should definitely consider writing and publishing a book. The leverage and instant expert status that comes along with being a published author is invaluable.

I know you may be thinking that you already have a marketing system that gets your message out and puts you in front of your target audience, but your competition is also using the same marketing methods. For instance you probably have a few lead generation methods like:

- A Website – Your competition has one too
- Business Cards – Your competition has them too
- PPC/Direct Mail Ads – Most of your competition is doing this as well
- Linkedin/Social Media Profiles – Yup, competition there
- Networking Events/Industry Conventions – You definitely have competition there
- Yellow Pages – Are you kidding me? No one uses those anymore

Publishing a book in your field gives you instant authority status which puts you above the crowd. People automatically perceive you as an expert because if you wrote a book about the subject then you must know something about it, right? Having your own book helps you to generate more leads; people read your book and contact you, and it will also help you close more deals, because again, you're the expert.

Consider this scenario for a moment, you're single and are seeking the assistance of a dating coach. You meet Karen at a meetup and she's friendly, knowledgeable, enthusiastic, compassionate, and empathetic to your needs. Before leaving the meetup, Karen gives you her business card with her phone number and website on it.

The following week you attend another meetup and this time you meet Cynthia. The two of you hit it off and she has similar qualities to the coach from last week. Before leaving she hands you a book that she is the author of titled: *Animal Magnetism: How to Attract Your Perfect Life Mate*. Of the two dating coaches, which one had the greatest impact? Which one are you going to remember? Do you even remember where you put what's-her-name's business card or have you already cracked open Cynthia's book and you're now using Karen's card as a bookmark?

Being a published author in your field gives you instant credibility, authority and expert status. People automatically see you as someone who knows what they're talking about and you stand out from the usual noise. You have leveraged yourself way ahead of the competition.

Your book really is the ultimate lead generation tool and you can give it away or use it as a source of additional income. Another awesome thing about having a book is that it can be distributed in physical form, as an eBook or even an audiobook. You can give it away in person or have readers/clients download the electronic format of their choice from the Internet.

Your book can also be used as a gateway to speaking opportunities, joint venture partnerships and give you exposure to other opportunities that you may not realize exist or have access to without having a published book.

Imagine the next time you're at an industry conference or networking event, you have a stack of books to handout while everyone else is passing out the usual stack of business cards. Can you imagine the possibilities and opportunities that book can bring you? Possible joint venture partners, new clients, referrals, media attention and more.

We are in an age in which the internet has opened up opportunities that weren't available to the average person just a few short years ago. Self-publishing portals have blown the lid off of the belief that only a select few can be authors, today anyone with the desire and a message can be an author and reach their audience.

If you have a message and a desire to spread that message then you should definitely write your book and have it published. If you have been in your profession for any significant amount of time, you have knowledge that your audience is looking for and. You could benefit from a book no matter what your profession or industry is. Here is a sample list of the industries and business types that could benefit from publishing a book:

- Accountants/CPAs
- Auto Mechanics
- Cake Designers
- Chiropractors
- Chefs
- Churches/Ministers

Get Your Bonus Gift…See Page 58

- Consultants/Coaches
- Cosmetologists
- Dentists
- Dieticians
- Event Planners
- Electricians
- Estheticians
- Financial Planners
- Foreign Language Experts
- Graphic Designers
- Home Improvement Specialists
- Insurance Agents
- Landscapers
- Loan Officers/Mortgage Brokers
- Massage Therapists
- Mental Health Professionals
- Network/Multi-level Marketers
- Nutrition Specialists
- Personal Trainers
- Photographers
- Physical/Occupational Therapists
- Real Estate Professionals
- Tutors
- Veterinarians
- Wedding Planners
- Insert Your Profession Here

Get Your Bonus Gift…See Page 58

Types of Books to Write

Ok, so now you see the value of writing a book for your business and industry, but what type of book would be the best fit? Well there are lots of books that you could write, but let's discuss the most effective types for the purpose of promoting your business as the ultimate lead generation tool. There are four book models that we'll describe here: How-To Books, Tip Books, Myth Busting Books and Interview-Style Books.

How-To Books

How-to books provide quality content to potential clients and customers and have a high perceived value. How-to information is some of the most frequently searched for information online. People are always trying to either find out how to do something or how to do something better.

For example if you are a wedding planner you could write a book about how to plan the perfect reception on a budget. A golf instructor could write a book about how to improve your swing in one weekend. An auto mechanic could write about how to make minor repairs on your car for the do-it-yourselfer. You know your industry inside and out so you have a great wealth of knowledge that your audience would love to know and is actively searching for.

The reason that how-to books are a great place to start is because you can focus on one aspect of your business, figure out what your core message is or what your audience's biggest problem/challenge is and you can write the entire book based around how to

Get Your Bonus Gift…See Page 58

solve that problem or challenge. Another reason how-to books are so powerful is because they can include graphs, charts and pictures to illustrate the steps which will help your readers to visualize the process and you also don't have to do a lot of writing. You can use the illustrations as a guide and write short precise instructions as to how to complete the steps.

By focusing on one topic or problem you are allowing your audience the opportunity to get to know, like and trust you. You are giving them the valuable information that they were looking for, you're building a relationship with them, and you are enhancing your perceived expert status in their mind so that when they need additional assistance you will be remembered.

Tip Books

Most people love to absorb small bits of information, all you have to do is give them what they want. You can write a short book with quick tips or small bits of a strategy to solve a problem or create an opportunity. For example if you're a dating coach you could write a "Top 7 Tips for Dating After a Divorce" and then fill it with seven short chapters, one for each tip that you have or a real estate agent could write "10 Tips Most First Time Home Buyers Never Consider" and again write ten chapters, one for each tip.

Now I know that it may sound insurmountable for to write an entire book but when you consider that a chapter only has to be the length of a really good article to be effective, it's really not that difficult to achieve. A well-researched and well-written article comes out to be about 1000 words which in a 6"x 9" print book or average kindle book is about 4 pages. At that rate 10 tips average out to be about 40 pages which is perfect for a business promotion, lead generation book.

A great resource that many professionals overlook is if you have maintained a business blog for any amount of time, then you already have the majority of the content you need for your book. You would only have to gather a collection of blog posts that are around the same topic, put them together so that they are in a coherent order and edit them into a tip style book. You may have to add some additional content to complete your book but the majority of the work is already done.

Myth-Busting Books

A myth-busting book is a book that is written to clarify and debunk common misconceptions about a particular topic in an industry or about the industry as a whole. For example an industry that has a lot of myths and misconceptions around it is network marketing, so a myth-busting network marketing book might be titled "Why Network Marketing is Not a Get Rich Quick Scheme and How You Can Make an Honest Living in Network Marketing" or a mental health myth-busting book might be titled "Everybody Isn't Popping Pills, Myths About Mental Health Treatment Demystified."

Just about every industry can write a myth-busting book because there are so many myths and misconceptions about anything and everything you can think of. There are myths and misconceptions about the real estate market, insurance costs, the safety of eating sushi, what gluten is and isn't, how dog food is made, acupuncture, what you can and can't do while pregnant…like I said pretty much everything.

Get Your Bonus Gift…See Page 58

All you would have to do is a little bit of research (most times just a simple *Google* search on myths about insert industry) and you'll find tons of material to write about.

Just like the tip book, the myth-busting book can be written around one specific topic in an industry and all of the myths about that topic. You can take 10, 20 or 30 myths about your industry and flesh each one out into the length of a well-written article and you have your book.

Interview Style Books

The last type of book we're going to discuss are interview style books. An interview style book is one where you write out a list of your 10 most frequently asked questions about your business or industry and then you write out the 10 questions that customers or clients should be asking.

The detailed answer to each of these twenty questions become a chapter of your book. Answering each question with as much detail as possible will give you more than enough content to create a book out of, and remember, If your answers come up short, a little research can go a long way towards completing your book.

How do I Write a Book if I'm Not a Writer

A common question from professionals is "how do I write a book if I'm not a writer?" and the answer is a lot simpler than you think. There are four methods for having your book written that I would recommend for the non-writer and they are; talk your book, record an interview & transcribe, have it ghostwritten and purchase a semi-custom/rebranded book.

This chapter will focus on describing these three methods of having your book written. Let's get started.

Talk Your Book

The first method is talk your book and it's as simple as it sounds. There are some awesome software programs out there that allow you to speak into a microphone plugged into your computer and the program will just type out the words you speak.

You could literally talk your book out into your computer. If you choose to do this, the program that I use and recommend is *Dragon NatuarallySpeaking* which you can get from nuance.com for around $100. It's a good investment if you plan on writing more than one book, if you plan on having a blog or improving one that you already have or if you just don't like to type things out.

Another suggestion if this is your chosen method is to outline the book using the table of contents. Once you have the table of contents under each chapter title, add 5 – 6 bullet points of topics that you will discuss for that chapter. When you're done with this outlining method you will have a clear picture of what your speaking points are.

Interview and Transcribe

The interview and transcribe method is when you get on the phone with a friend or colleague and record them asking you questions that you have written out in the form of an interview and then you answer each of the questions in great detail.

This is also the perfect method to use for FAQ/SAQ questions to create a book. FAQs are the most frequently asked questions you get from your customers and clients or the most frequently asked questions about your profession or business industry. SAQs are the questions you feel your customers and clients should be asking.

These questions don't have to be written in fancy language because no one will ever see them. Your questions only need to be written in a way that prompts your thoughts and gets you talking.

You don't even necessarily need to have anyone interview you, if you have a voice recorder (most smart phones come equipped with them) or a microphone that plugs into your computer, you could simply answer each question on your list in detail, right into the recording device.

Once you have recorded the entire list of questions and detailed answers, you have the audio transcribed and edited into a manuscript that you can have published.

There are some very inexpensive places to have your audio transcribed online. You could try rev.com, fiverr.com or do a *Google* search for audio transcription services to find someone to outsource the job to if you don't have in-house staff to do the work.

Have it Ghostwritten

Having your book ghostwritten is a fairly easy process. You can find ghostwriters online pretty easily at hirewriters.com, elance.com or *Google* ghostwriters to find talented writers.

You submit the job description, writers respond with offer bids, you choose one, have your book written and published. Pretty simple right. But what if you don't want the entire book ghostwritten? In that case you could hire a ghostwriter to just write any number of relevant articles that you need to complete your book.

You give them the criteria, such as topic, word length and the number of articles you need and pay once they're written. If you choose to use this method make sure that you request original work and exclusive rights to the work so that you don't have the same content as someone else, you may also want to request a sample of their work to assist in making your hiring decision.

Once you receive your articles you put them together with your other content in a logical order, edit where necessary and have your book published.

Purchase Semi-Custom/ReBranded Books

Semi-custom or rebranded books (also known as private label rights books or PLR) are books that have been completely written by someone else about a subject in your niche or industry that you can purchase the rights to use for your own book.

Get Your Bonus Gift…See Page 58

Changes would have to be made to customize the book to your particular business but the bulk of the work is already done. When you purchase the private label rights to someone else's book you have the right to change the content inside the book, change the graphics and cover art and also to put your name on the book and claim authorship to the book.

There are many different types of rights or licensing that you can have when purchasing PLR material so make sure you read the rights sheet very carefully if you intend to go this route so that you are clear as to what you do and do not have the rights to do with the material.

Any of these methods work will work for the four types of books that we discussed earlier and probably any other book model that you may consider for writing your business promotion book. So as you can see, you don't have to be a writer to have a book to promote your business and generate leads.

Putting Your Book Together

We have discussed why you need a book, what types of books you could write and how to write a book even if you're not a writer. Now let's discuss how to put your book together so that you can use it to promote your business and generate leads.

There are five sections that we need to discuss in order for you to complete your book; the title, the cover, the look and feel of the content, editing and formatting the book for print on demand (POD) publishing.

The Title

The title is your book's headline, it's the element that makes someone pick up your book and look at it. You have to draw your potential customers and clients in with the title otherwise they'll never see the inside of your book or read your message.

The title should be something catchy but more important it should speak directly to your target audience by incorporating keywords that they are already searching for.

If you don't know what a keyword is, it's the word or phrase that people type into any search engine when they're looking for something. For example the keywords for the book you're reading are "publish your book" and "promote your business." So when someone does a search on *Google* or *Amazon* for how to promote a business or how to publish a business book, my book will show up in the search results.

There are tons of books and tutorials out there to teach you all about keyword research and optimization, but that is out of the scope of this particular book so again, the short answer for what is a keyword is simply the words or phrase that people type in when they're looking for something.

So in order to create a title that speaks to your target audience, you have to consider first what your topic is and second what would your target audience type in if they were looking for a solution to a problem that your book or business can solve.

For instance if I wanted to buy a house with bad credit and no money down, I would go to *Google* and type in "how to buy a house with bad credit and no money down" and if there was a book with the title "How to Buy a House With Bad Credit and No Money Down", it should show up in the search results.

Your goal when creating the title for your book is to give your audience what they want by following the path of least resistance. If you are writing a real estate book and you want to attract bad credit, no money down buyers you don't want to name your book " How to Buy REOs in Anytown, USA" because a title like that isn't going to get you very many views. Why? Well first of all the average person doesn't know what an REO is, so they aren't going to be searching for them and second the search engines have no way of knowing that you want your book to show up for bad credit , no money down searchers because you haven't told them. So your book with its REO title will only show up when someone is actively searching for REOs which again, the average person never searches for.

Get Your Bonus Gift…See Page 58

Your title should convey a benefit to the reader and again whenever possible have their keyword in it. So it would look something like these (I'll give you four formulas you can use):

1. How to [Do whatever your target audience is trying to figure out how to do] - How to Get Rid of Back Pain Without Drugs
2. Tips on [Whatever your target audience needs or wants advice about] – Tips on Grooming Your Cocker Spaniel like The Pros.
3. The Truth About [Whatever your target audience has misconceptions or believes myths about] – The Truth About Curing Infertility With Acupuncture
4. Questions You Should Ask [Professional] Before You [Whatever your target audience is thinking about doing] – Questions You Should Ask Your Dentist Before You Let Your Teen Get Braces

Clearly, these are not the only formulas for coming up with great book titles. They are just provided to get your creative juices flowing.

The Cover

Just like the title, the cover needs to get the attention of your target audience. I'm sorry to say that ugly book covers hurt sales, badly. Let's face it we all judge books by their cover, it's just in our nature to be drawn to things that are visually appealing.

Get Your Bonus Gift…See Page 58

There are a number of ways to get a professional looking cover for your book.

1. You could try to create it yourself - if you know how to use graphic design software I say go for it, but if not I wouldn't recommend this option.
2. You could hire a professional graphics designer – this option is an expensive one.
3. You could go on fiverr.com – there are some very talented people on fiverr and for the price, it's an awesome choice. Just be careful because you get what you pay for and sometimes you have to go through 4 or 5 different artists before you find the perfect fit.

Again, these aren't the only options. You can do a search on *Google* for book cover designers and/or book cover templates.

The Look and Feel of Your Content

We've spent a lot of time covering the types of books that you could write and how to come up with content, how to organize your content and how to add to it if necessary. Now let's talk about the look and feel of the interior of your book.

Your book should be typed in a font that is easy to read and is pleasant to look at. You should not use a font that is too designer oriented, there are many fonts that look cool and would be great for graphic design but they just don't work for writing books. You should stick to something in the sans or sans serif font families like Times New Roman, Arial, Calibri or Verdana. These fonts are great for book writing. There are others that will work just as well, use your own judgment and taste to choose a font that is right for your book. One more note, generally as a rule of thumb, your font size should be no larger than 12 pts.

Editing

Now editing is a subject that no one gets excited about (unless you're a professional editor), but it is something that every book needs to make sure that it is clear, focused and without grammatical errors.

You may choose to hire a professional editor which is perfectly fine, and just like hiring ghostwriters, there are online resources where you can find editors fairly inexpensively. Check out: elance.com, odesk.com or do a *Google* search for freelance book editors for more options.

You can also request the assistance of a family member, friend or colleague in editing your book, and there are lots of students available through *Craigslist* that offer editing services. If you can't find one in your area you can place an ad for one in the jobs/gigs section, I'm sure you'll get more than enough replies to get your editing done.

Most often writers will self-edit their work which will also work just fine for our purposes (and it's pretty easy when you write in Microsoft Word, those red and blue squiggly lines are very helpful). Self-editing can be done chapter by chapter or all at once when your manuscript is done.

Either way you should edit your book a few times, taking breaks in between so that you can go over your book with fresh eyes.

The first time you go over your book focus on the clarity of it. Because you know everything about your profession and business, your explanations in the book may make perfect sense to you but confuse your reader.

Have someone read it for you and get their feedback. Things to have them look for are whether or not the writing is clear and where they get confused. Have them read it to you out loud to help show the confusing parts or where something may be misread.

The second time you go through editing your book, check for the use of verbs. Get rid of as many passive verbs as possible and replace them with action and action-oriented verbs.

Your editing goal is to make sure the information is presented in a clear, logical and user-friendly way. These are the things you should have your editor look for if you decide to hire someone to edit your manuscript. Use the replace function in MS word and target words like; is, was, had, has, could, are, etc.

If you can, try to replace these with action verbs like; look, feel, sound, appear, prove, grow, etc.

Finally read it aloud and listen for bumps and glitches. See if you misread anything, notice where the words or sentences trip you up or cut off in an awkward place or breaks the flow of the paragraph. Also, see if there are any elements that just don't sound right, and either tweak them or delete them.

Get Your Bonus Gift…See Page 58

Formatting Your Manuscript for POD Publishing

A common mistake that people make when self-publishing their book is to leave the page size to the default 8.5" x 11" when writing. If you setup the interior dimensions of your book from the beginning, by setting your document to the exact trim size that you will ultimately publish your book in, you won't have to try to recalculate the pages and reconfigure the margins once you're ready to print.

The average lead generating book trim size would be 5.5" x 8" or 6" x 9". We will setup the interior dimensions for a 6" x 9" book. So inside MS Word open a new document and click on the page layout tab at the top.

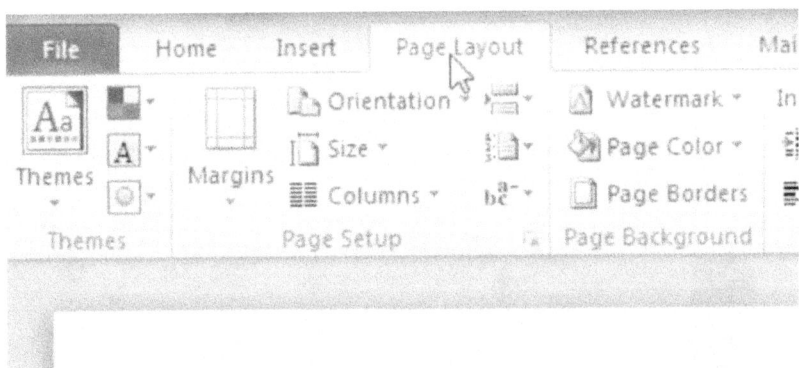

Then click on size,

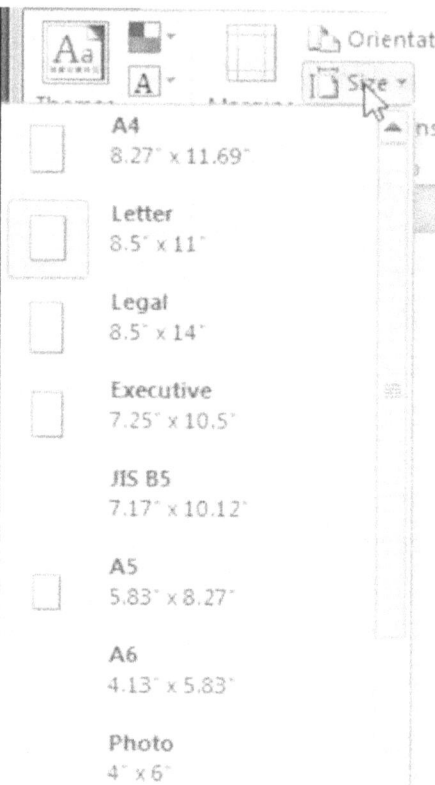

Then scroll down to the bottom of that menu and click on more paper sizes,

On this screen you'll enter the height and width based on your book's final trim size.

Then you will click on the margins tab and enter 0.7 for the top, bottom, inside and outside. Then you will enter 0.35 for the gutter and then click OK.

Get Your Bonus Gift...See Page 58

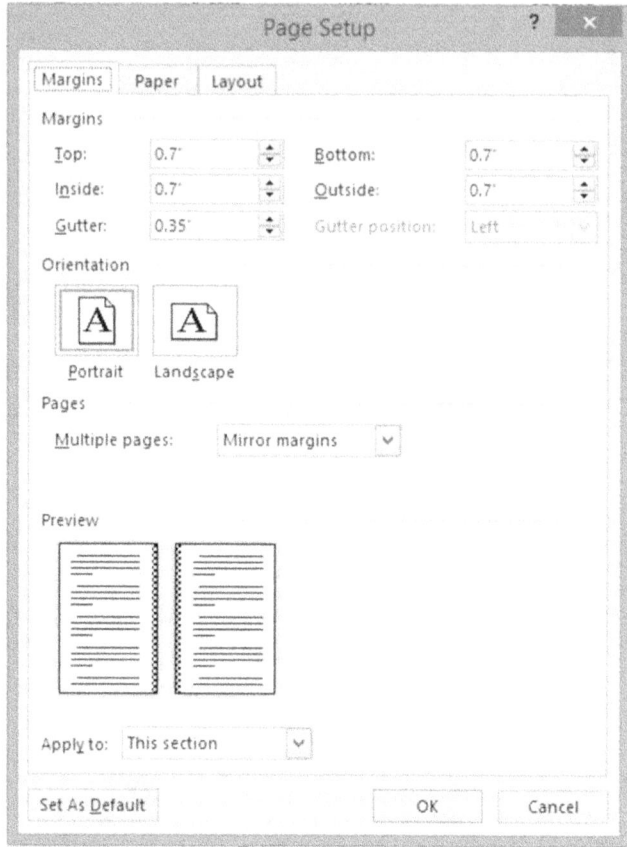

Once you click OK, you have your document setup to the trim size that you will eventually publish your book in.

Setting up your book's interior dimensions ahead of time also goes a long way in helping you to keep up with how many pages you've written so far and how many pages your final manuscript will be. One final thing you want to set from the beginning is the header and page numbering of your book. To do this click on the insert tab.

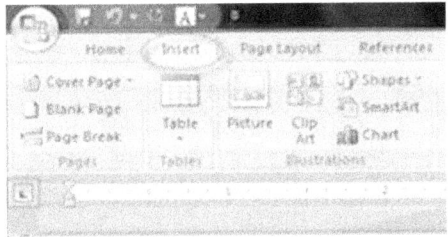

Then you can go through the available header, footer and page number options. It is common to add the name of the book and author to the header and the page number to the footer of the page. If you don't want to have the header show up on page one select the different first page option under header, edit header, options section.

Once your manuscript is complete you will want to create a PDF document to upload to the POD publisher. To ensure that your page settings remain intact you will need to either click file, print and select PDF under your available printers.

Get Your Bonus Gift…See Page 58

Then you will provide a name and location for the PDF document to be saved.

If PDF isn't an option under printers you will click on file, export and select create PDF/xps document.

Then provide a name and location for the exported document. To make sure that all of your settings, photos, etc. are embedded you need to check the PDF settings that will be used to create your PDF file. If available, select "PDF/X-1a," "High-Quality Print" or "Press Quality" from the list of presets, then click Export or OK.

Get Your Bonus Gift…See Page 58

Now Is the Perfect Time to Publish Your Book

Now is the perfect time to publish your business promotion book and use it to generate unlimited leads for your business. Companies like *Amazon, Barnes & Noble and Apple* have not only made it possible to publish your own books, but have also made the process fairly easy. Anyone who desires to have a published book or become a published author now has the opportunity to do so without the hassle and restriction of using agents and large publishing houses.

Amazon's print on demand platform: *CreateSpace* allows you to retain ownership of the copyright of your book and lists you on *Amazon*.com without any fees or additional work on your behalf. *CreateSpace* is the most popular and easiest to use of the three so that is where we will focus our efforts.

Setting Up Your CreateSpace Account

The first step to publishing your business promotion book is to setup an account with *CreateSpace* to do that go to www.createspace.com and click on Signup:

Get Your Bonus Gift…See Page 58

Then you will be required to fill-in your account information in the form on the next page:

Create a New Account

* Email Address yourname@email.com
This will be used as your Login ID.

* Password ••••••••

* Re-Enter ••••••••
Let's make sure you typed that right.

* First Name Your First Name

* Last Name Your Last Name

* Country
United States

* What type of media are you considering publishing?
Book

Request a free consultation to learn about our professional fee-based publishing services ☐

Send me Updates and Promotions ☑
We won't sell your contact information. Privacy Policy

Create My Account

Get Your Bonus Gift…See Page 58

Once you submit the form you will come to the Membership Agreement page, read the terms, check I agree and click on the continue button.

Once you click continue, you will be immediately taken to your CreateSpace member's dashboard:

Get Your Bonus Gift…See Page 58

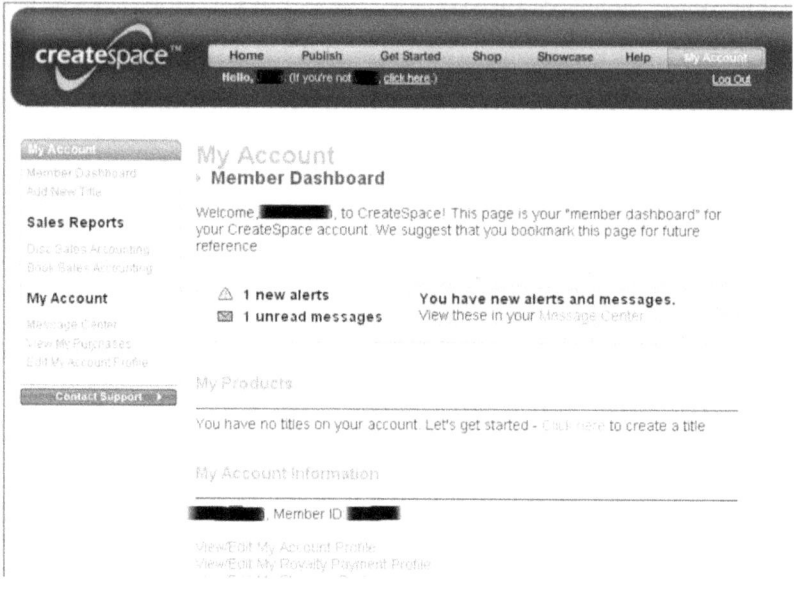

Adding Your Book To Your Account

The next thing you'll need to do is add your book and publishing information to your account for approval. The following is a step by step overview of the process.

Click on the Add New Title link on your dashboard:

Page | 31

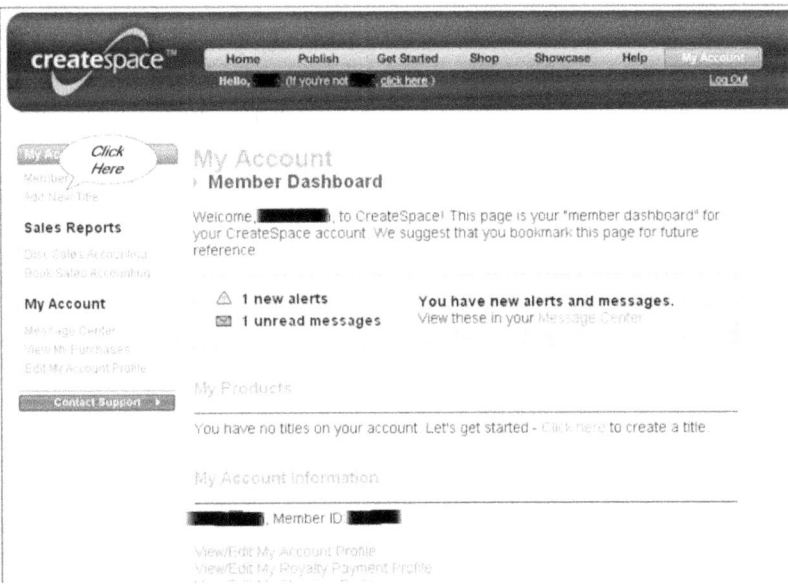

On your new project page enter the title of your book, select paperback and choose the guided setup process:

Next you will enter your book's information including subtitle, author name, etc.:

Get Your Bonus Gift...See Page 58

Next you will choose your ISBN settings. An ISBN is basically a book's identification number, it registers the title, author and publisher to a specific book and can not be changed. It is needed in order to publish and distribute your book. *CreateSpace* will assign an ISBN number for your book free of charge, which is just fine for our purposes.

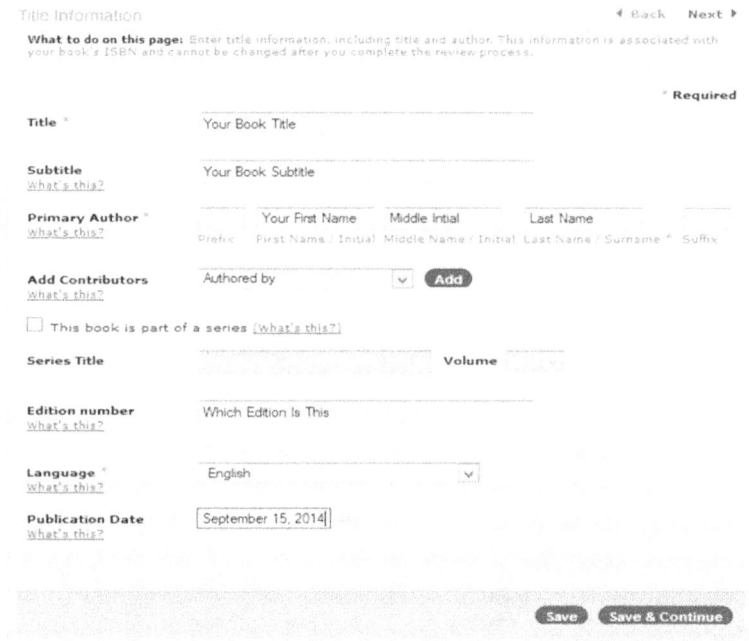

There are three other options you can choose from as well. Custom ISBN allows you to put your company name as the publisher of your book, the price is $10. Custom Universal ISBN allows you to choose the name of the publisher as well as having more distribution options. Provide Your Own ISBN allows you to use an ISBN number that you purchased from a ISBN broker but haven't already assigned to another book.

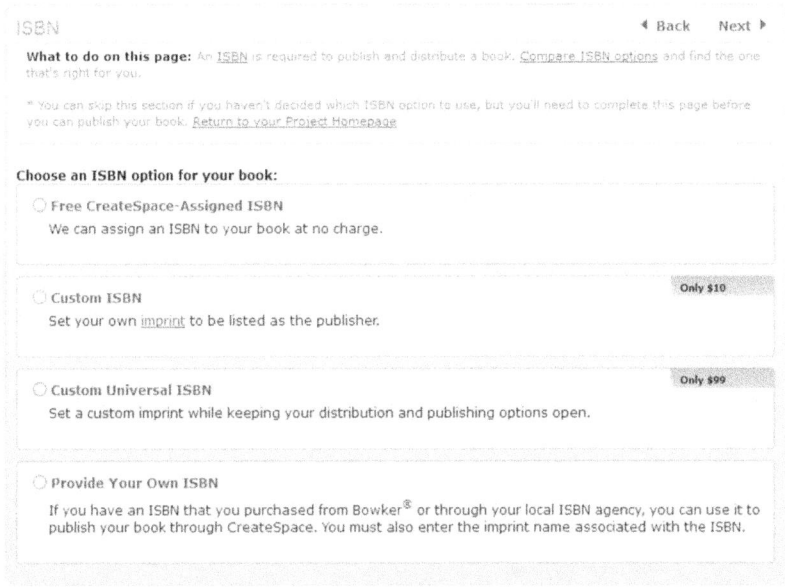

Once you've made your selection click continue. Next you will select your interior details like black and white or color, trim size and how you would like to submit the interior of your book . The trim size is the dimensions of your book, there are 12 industry-standard trim sizes including 5 x 8, 6 x 9, 7 x 10 and 8 x 11. This book is 6 x 9, which is the most popular trim size for a business book. You can also download a template for the trim size you choose under the trim size option on this page.

Get Your Bonus Gift...See Page 58

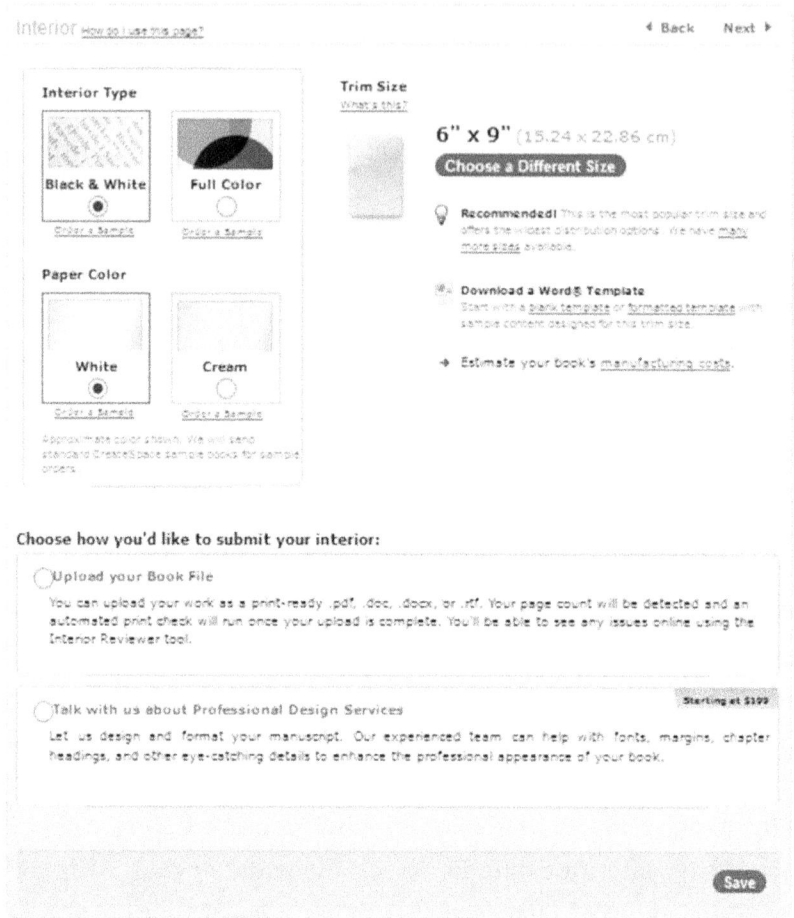

The next step is to decide on cover options. You have the option of having a matte cover or glossy cover printed. Then you make your choice between designing your book cover with the *CreateSpace Cover Creator* which can be launched from this page once you click on the Build Your Cover Online option, you can pay to have your book cover professionally designed or you can upload a PDF of the cover you have already designed yourself or had outsourced to a freelancer.

Get Your Bonus Gift…See Page 58

Designing The Cover

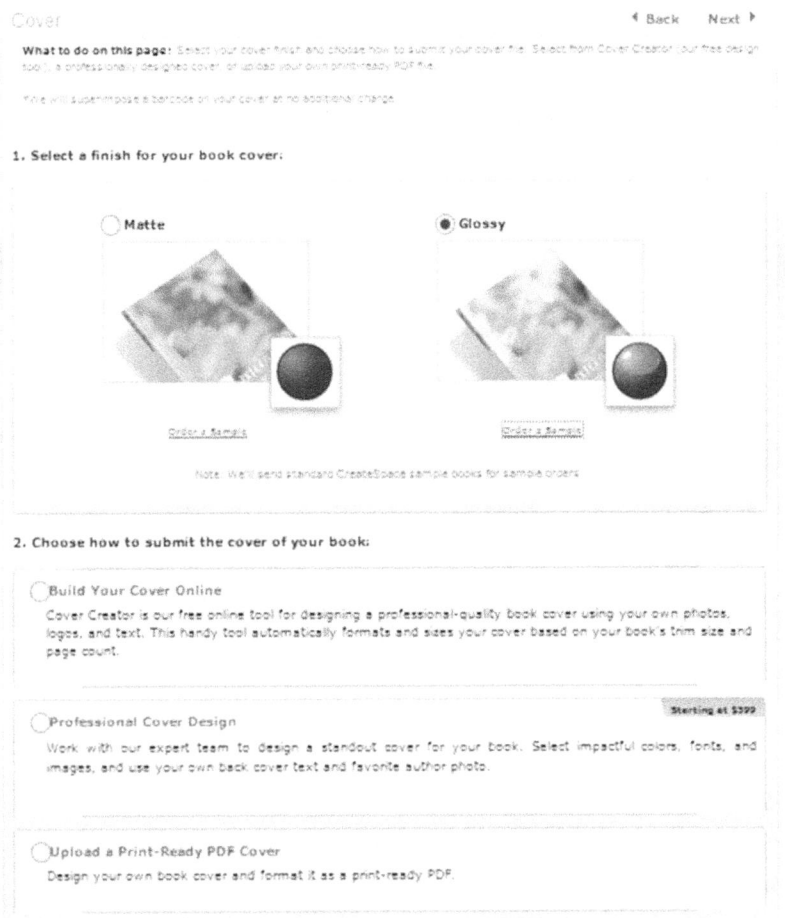

It's actually very easy to create your cover using the *CreateSpace* Cover Creator, and it's the perfect option to choose for no hassle book cover design and creation. It is also the quickest option to get your book done.

The Cover Creator has 30 different cover styles, over 2,000 images to choose from and plenty of font themes. The great thing about this tool is that you don't have to worry about getting the formatting right because it's done automatically for you.

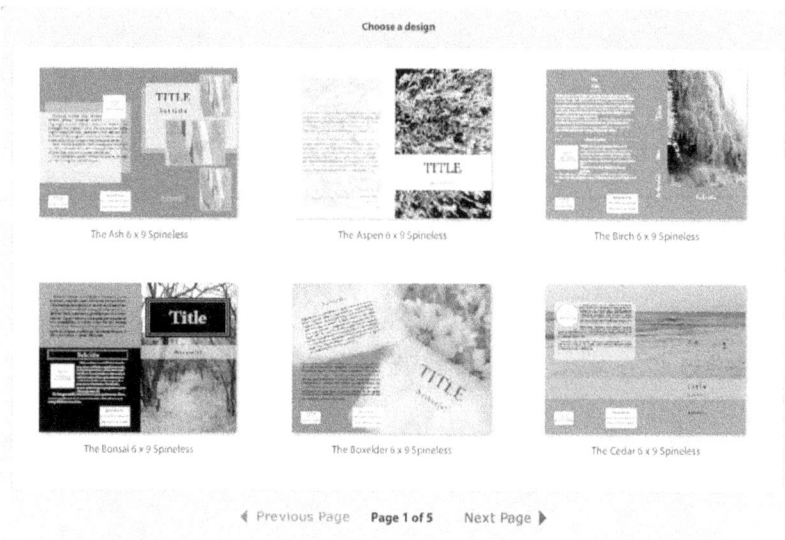

I recommend using the Cover Creator because it's simple to use and will allow you to get your book done quickly so that you can begin using it to generate leads a lot sooner.

If you would like to design your own cover or have it outsourced as opposed to using the Cover Creator, you can download the cover template from this link:
https://www.createspace.com/Help/Book/Artwork.do

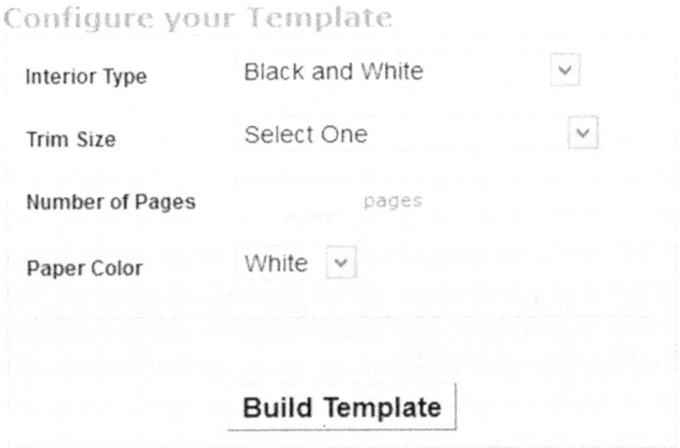

Configure your Template

Interior Type	Black and White
Trim Size	Select One
Number of Pages	pages
Paper Color	White

Build Template

There you configure the template by filling out the options form. They ask for your interior type, trim size, the number of pages and your paper color choice.

The optimal choices for your lead generation book are black and white interior and a trim size of 6 X 9. Once you click on Build Template, you will be taken to a page where you can download your template in a .zip file.

Get Your Bonus Gift…See Page 58

The cover file is a wrap-around file that consists of the front cover, back cover and the spine of the book. Here's an example of how the finished cover will look:

Get Your Bonus Gift…See Page 58

Once you have completed your cover design, you need to save it as a PDF file (if you outsource to a cover designer make sure you receive the finished cover as a PDF file) and upload it into your *CreateSpace* account.

Another thing you need to consider when hiring a professional cover designer is the content for the back cover. Include a short author biography, a short blurb describing what the book is about and your website address.

Once you submit your files and look through your book in the interior reviewer to make sure it looks the way you intended before you submit your files for review. Once you submit your files for review it can take up to 24 hours to be complete. Once your book is approved you can order a proof copy.

When you receive your printed proof copy in the mail, proof-read the book, and have some friends, family members or colleagues to proof-read the copy as well. Take note of any irregularities in the layout and pictures. If everything is to your liking, you can approve your proof. Once approved, your book will be immediately available to order from the *CreateSpace.com* website.

Choose Your Distribution Channels

Once you have submitted your file for review you will have the opportunity to choose the distribution channels for your book. By default the standard distribution options are already selected. (*Amazon.com, Amazon Europe & CreateSpace eStore*)

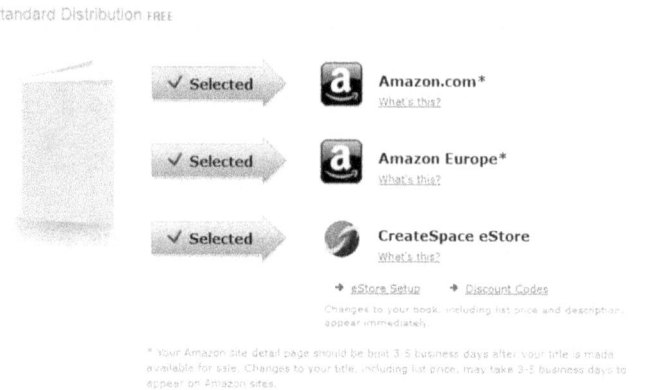

Then you have the option to select expanded distribution options which include *CreateSpace Direct,* which makes your books available to certified resellers such as independent bookstores and book resellers; Bookstores and Online Retailers, which makes your book available to thousands of major online and offline bookstores and retailers, and increase the potential audience for your books; and Libraries and Academic Institutions, which makes your book available to public libraries, elementary and secondary school libraries, and libraries at other academic institutions.

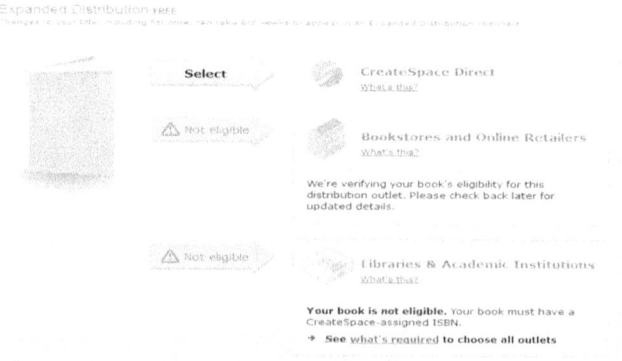

Get Your Bonus Gift...See Page 58

After you make your distribution selections, it's time to determine the price for your book. *CreateSpace* has a pricing tool which will show you what your royalty is from sales on your standard distribution channels based on the price you set for your book.

Here's the royalty break down for a book priced at $15.97.

Next you will fill in the description of your book using your keywords to help your book show up in the Amazon search for the phrases your audience would use. You will also select the category your book will be listed in, add an author biography, book language, country of publication and again select search keywords.

Get Your Bonus Gift…See Page 58

Once this is complete you will just wait for the review process to be completed and then order a proof copy of your book.

When you receive your proof copy make sure that you read through your book to make sure no grammar errors were missed, to make sure that your book looks the way you intended for it to look and to check for any other mishaps that may have occurred.

Again you may want to request the assistance of a family member, friend or colleague to look and read through the proof copy to make sure you haven't missed or overlooked anything that needs correcting. Once you are happy with you book, approve it in your *CreateSpace* account and it will be available for sale on *Amazon* in 3-5 days.

Get Your Bonus Gift…See Page 58

Enhancing Your Credibility Through Book Promotion

There are a lot of reasons to promote your book, like to make sales that generate additional income, to get your book to bestseller's status and to enhance to your credibility as an expert.

Additional income is great but you shouldn't expect that income to be substantial and it's not the primary goal of publishing your book anyway. Getting your book to bestseller's status goes a long way towards enhancing your credibility and should be one of your primary goals. Your primary goal through book promotion is to enhance your credibility as an expert.

Enhancing your credibility helps take away any objections your potential clients may have when making the decision to hire you or purchase from you over your competitors. There are five methods of book promotion that I recommend, they are book reviews, a dedicated book site, press releases, video marketing and social media marketing. We will discuss these methods here.

Book Reviews

The first step in enhancing your credibility is to get book reviews. Having reviews on your book's listing page shows that other people are reading your book and adds value to your work. Honest book reviews are a lot like testimonials for your book, and positive honest reviews are like getting a recommendation from readers that encourage your potential clients and customers to work with you.

Get Your Bonus Gift…See Page 58

There are a number of ways to get book reviews for your book very early in the publishing process. One way is to send the PDF version along with the link to your *Amazon* listing to family, friends and non-competitive colleagues and ask them to read the book and leave an honest review on your *Amazon* book page.

Another way would be to send the first two chapters to your electronic mailing list with an offer stating that if they would read those two chapters and leave you an honest review on *Amazon* that you will give them the entire book in PDF format once the review is posted.

You could do a *Google* search for non-fiction book reviewers or "your topic" book reviewers and follow their submission guidelines to get them to read and review your book. The last way I recommend you get early book reviews is to go to Fiverr.com and search for Amazon book reviews or Amazon verified book reviews. Once you find listings that you are interested in, read their gig description and make sure they will provide honest reviews.

Avoid listings that offer guaranteed five star ratings because you want honest, legitimate and ethical reviews. A guaranteed five star review will most likely be spammy and will just hurt your book's credibility in the end.

To further make sure that the reviewers you choose to work with on *Fiverr* are providing honest quality reviews you could send them a question asking if they will actually read your book before leaving a review. It is important that they do this because you are paying them $5 for their time to actually read your book, not to leave spam reviews on *Amazon*.

Dedicated Book Site

Promoting your book with a dedicated book site is great for getting your book noticed by your potential customers and clients. You can use it to get your book listed on *Google* using keywords. You can pre-sell your book by writing good promotional copy on the site with a link back to your book on *Amazon* so that your visitors can purchase your book.

You can't add promotional copy to your book listing on *Amazon* because it's against their terms and conditions, so having a dedicated book site gives you the ability to promote your book however you want.

You can use your book site as a lead generating tool by allowing visitors to download a free chapter of your book in exchange for their name and email address. You can add some reviews and testimonials on your site either from your current customers or some of the reviews that are listed on your book listing page on *Amazon*.

You can add an about the author section that lists some information about you and you can add links from your book site out to other products or services that you may have so you can do some cross promoting.

Amazon doesn't allow you to put outgoing links on your book listing page, so having your own dedicated book site gives you the flexibility to promote more than just your book, you can promote whatever you want because it's your site.

You can also add book promotion videos on your site to further pre-sell your book because people love to watch videos and if they

Get Your Bonus Gift…See Page 58

are engaging enough you will generate interest to your book and your business.

Press Releases

Press releases are one of the most effective promotional methods around. A well written press release will generate backlinks to your website as well as help to generate sales of your book.

The backlinks that are generated from your press release will help your book show up for relevant keyword searches in *Google* which helps your target audience find your book and your business when they are looking for a solution to a problem they may have.

There is a formula to writing good press releases and I believe it is more of an art form than anything else so in this section I am going to recommend that you outsource the writing of your press release if you aren't experienced in writing them yourself.

Once again we're going to go to fiverr.com and search for press release, then sort by rating or popularity to find the top gigs. First select a press release writer that offers at least 200 – 350 word press releases and follow their instructions for hiring them.

Once you receive your newly written press release go back to fiverr.com and search for press release distribution. Sort again by either popularity or rating and select one that offers to send your release to at least 25 media outlets. Have your release distributed and you're done.

Video Marketing

You can create a book promotion video fairly easily and upload it to *YouTube* to generate traffic back to your book listing. You can use *Camtasia* or *Jing* along with *PowerPoint* to create a nice, attractive and effective book promotion video.

Create a *PowerPoint* presentation describing some key themes in your book and then record the presentation in *Camtasia* or *Jing* into a 5 minute video. If you don't know how to use this method to create videos you could always outsource your video creation on fiverr.com as well, just search for PowerPoint video creation.

After you upload it to your *YouTube,* account give your video a title that targets the keywords used by your target audience (e.g. Your Ultimate Lead Generation Tool) and then write a keyword rich description about your video. Make sure you front load your description with the link to your book listing page on *Amazon.*

If you have multiple articles around the topic of your book that you didn't use in your book they would be the perfect content to turn into videos. As I stated before, you can just highlight the most important points in each article and put them into a *PowerPoint* presentation and record short promotional videos with a link in the description of each one pointing to your book listing page to drive up sales.

You could even put a link to your dedicated book site promoting the free chapter download if you are trying to increase the size of your mailing list. To get views to your videos you can go back to fiverr.com and do a search for YouTube views and purchase some video views from a couple of the providers on there.

Get Your Bonus Gift...See Page 58

The reason you want to get views to your videos is because having multiple views helps increase the popularity of your video and helps the chances of your video showing up in the top listings for your keywords when potential customers search for them.

One last note on video marketing, you can also use a service like tubemogul.com to upload your videos to multiple video sharing sites in addition to *YouTube* for additional traffic to your book listing page, your book site and/or your business website.

Social Media Marketing

Social media is an awesome way to promote your new book and generate interest in readership and possibly attract new clients and customers.

The first thing you will want to do is create a *Facebook* page for your book and in the website section put the link to your book listing page. You will need to invite all of your friends to "like" your new page and begin adding content to your page immediately.

You can add posts highlighting some of the key points in your book with a link to download a free chapter on your dedicated book site. You can post some of your YouTube video links on your page, and you can post links to articles on your business website that are around the same topic as your book to drive traffic to your main site.

Just make sure that you are posting new content to your book page on *Facebook* at least a few times a week if not every day, and make sure that your posts are relevant and helpful content, not just spammy buy my book posts.

Get Your Bonus Gift…See Page 58

Next you will want to list your new book in the overview section of your *Linkedin* account with a link to your *Amazon* book listing page. Then just as with *Facebook,* post relevant article links, video links and offers for the free chapter download on your own status updates a few times a week.

Always make sure that you aren't spamming your friends and connections on social media sites so that you don't lose your credibility.

These are the five methods that I recommend you use to promote your book to generate traffic, leads and sales online.

Get Your Bonus Gift…See Page 58

Generating Leads With Your Book

Now for the part I now you've been waiting for, how to generate leads with your new book. Amazon makes it very easy and affordable for you to purchase copies of your own book for around $4 + shipping per copy. Go into your dashboard and order a few copies of your book and give them away to customers, colleagues, and potential clients.

Have copies on hand when you go to networking meetings and industry events to give away to people there. Make sure you have contact information inside your book or a business card slid in each copy as a bookmark.

To build a list of potential clients online use your pdf file as an eBook and give it away in exchange for their name and email address so that you can follow up with them with maybe an offer of your services, a coupon for a product or a consultation.

In the footer of your book or on a special page in the back make sure to add an offer for a free bonus of some kind that is related to your business and the book that you have written.

Setup a special webpage for the readers of your book to go and give you their name and email address in exchange for something related to your book that would be of value to them. For example, a buyer's guide to the type of service you offer. If you are a plumber it could be 10 tips to hiring the best plumber for your job. You

Get Your Bonus Gift…See Page 58

could offer a consumer awareness guide for something in your industry that most people don't know to look out for. Again, it could be a special coupon for an exclusive discount on a product or service only offered to the readers of your book.

Once your readers have requested their bonus you could send them to an upsell page where they have an opportunity to purchase a product or signup for a training course or other type of service right then while they are still in buying mode and warmed to your offer. You may have a course that is an expanded training on the information you gave them in the bonus or an upgrade to the product or service that you gave them a coupon for.

You could purchase a mailing list of potential clients and create a postcard campaign offering a free copy of your book with your book website listed on the postcard. When interested potential clients visit your website they'll fill in the request form with their mailing information, effectively telling you that they are indeed interested in your product or service and giving you permission to contact them further. You could even setup a free plus shipping offer to cover the cost of mailing them the book.

Another great way to generate leads with your book is to distribute a press release that promotes the free plus shipping book offer website. Those who respond to the offer are very interested leads for your business.

You can setup a webinar using your book as an outline of content to speak about and offer an electronic copy of your book as a bonus to all registrants who attend your webinar to the end.

Get Your Bonus Gift…See Page 58

You can also generate leads by creating a book trailer video or having the video created by a freelancer and then uploading the book trailer video to video sharing sites like *YouTube or Vimeo,* and promoting your free plus shipping book offer website in the video description section.

Finally, you can use your book as an offer to begin a joint venture partnership with a colleague who may be in the same field as you but isn't a direct competitor, someone who may offer a complimentary product or service to those you offer. For example if you are a massage therapist you may want to joint venture with an esthetician.

You could make an offer to promote a product or service of theirs in exchange for them displaying your book in their business or giving away copies of the book to their clients and customers.

There are quite a few ways that you can use your new book as a lead generator. Your book can be your gateway to speaking appearances, media publicity, interviews on radio stations and podcasts. You are only limited by your own imagination.

Just remember that the primary goal of your book is to be a leveraging and lead generation tool. If you make some sales that is awesome, but it isn't the goal. Use it to build up your database of customers, clients and potential joint venture partners.

Take Action Now

We have discussed why you want to write and publish a book, what types of books to write and how to write a book if you're not a writer. We have gone step by step through the process of setting up your account with CreateSpace, uploading your book, creating your cover and publishing your new ultimate lead generating tool. We have talked about how to generate leads with your book and even how to potentially get a joint venture partner or two from your book.

Now it is time for you to take action and actually get to writing and publishing your book. I am thrilled that you picked up my book and read it but it means nothing if you don't actually put the advice to work for you in your business.

If you get just one new customer or client from the methods that I have laid out in these pages then I have done my job and my goal has been accomplished. I thank you for spending some time with me…Now it's time for you to act.

Go publish your book.

About The Author

Author, consultant, and online marketing professional V. LaTonya Cobbs is an expert at helping small businesses and independent professionals gain a dominant position in their local marketplace.

V. LaTonya specializes in helping entrepreneurs, small businesses and independent professionals gain a competitive advantage in their market both online and off. She makes sure that these businesses are able to be found online, ensures that they never run out of leads, and helps them to transform potential clients into lifetime customers (and raving fans!)

If you are serious about improving your business' bottom line and would like to schedule a free consultation to see how V. LaTonya can help you create and publish your lead generating book or setup a comprehensive online marketing campaign for your company, you can contact her by leaving your name, telephone number and email address at www.ArevMediaMarketingConsultants.com, or by leaving a voicemail message at 513.601.8075

V. LaTonya is the author of several business and marketing books on Amazon and you can visit her at www.ArevMediaMarketingConsultants.com

V. LaTonya Cobbs lives in Cincinnati, Oh with her son DaVon, a bi-polar Cocker Spaniel named Oreo and two very talkative Tabby cats named Divine & Polka Dots.

Get Your Bonus Gift…See Page 58

Have the Author Speak at Your Next Event

Want to have the author speak at your next event?
Our programs are designed to optimize lead generation and online marketing strategies for professionals, entrepreneurs and small business owners.

Our agency focuses on leveraging your knowledge and expertise in your field by educating your market using a variety of content delivery methods including video, social media, different forms of text based content and a few others, as an alternative to traditional marketing.

Our educational speaking topics include:

- How to Publish Your Own Book for Lead Generation and Business Promotion
- How to Generate Leads Promote Your Business and with Social Media
- How to Promote Your Business and Generate Leads Using Mobile Marketing

To request a full list of speaking topics or to book the author at your next speaking event visit: www.ArevMediaMarketingConsultants.com/contact-us

Done-For-You Book Service

Although I honest believe that anyone can write and publish their own business promoting and lead generating book (and they should), I know that small business owners are busy with the everyday tasks that it takes to run a business.

I also believe in the lead generating power of having your own book and the leverage it can bring you over your competition, which is why I have created "done for you packages" to help you not only have your book written but published and in some instances marketed as well.

We offer several packages designed to fit most any budget and still provide you with high quality service that will pay for itself in multiple times. If you know the value of a new customer for your business then you will agree that having a tool that pre-sells your target audience, qualifies them and brings them to you is well worth the investment.

Some examples of the services we provide are: book writing, formatting & publishing (or formatting & publishing if your book is already written), book selling site creation, book marketing site creation, podcast creation, video marketing page, and more.

For a free consultation go to:
www.AreuMediaMarketingConsultants.com

Get Your Bonus Gift…See Page 58

Readers Only Bonus

I want you to know that I really appreciate you taking the time to read my book so I have an exclusive readers only bonus for you...

Register Your Copy of This Book and Get a Free Mobile Website to Promote Your New Book and Generate Leads as a Bonus.

Go to: www.PublishYourBookPromoteYourBusiness.com/bonus

Get Your Bonus Gift...See Page 58

www.ingramcontent.com/pod-product-compliance
Lightning Source LLC
Chambersburg PA
CBHW071807170526
45167CB00003B/1209